PRINCEWILL LAGANG

The Ambani Empire: Mukesh Ambani's Journey to Business Mastery

First published by PRINCEWILL LAGANG 2023

Copyright © 2023 by Princewill Lagang

All rights reserved. No part of this publication may be reproduced, stored or transmitted in any form or by any means, electronic, mechanical, photocopying, recording, scanning, or otherwise without written permission from the publisher. It is illegal to copy this book, post it to a website, or distribute it by any other means without permission.

Princewill Lagang asserts the moral right to be identified as the author of this work.

First edition

This book was professionally typeset on Reedsy.
Find out more at reedsy.com

Contents

1	Introduction	1
2	The Genesis of Ambani Dominance	3
3	Building Blocks of the Ambani Empire: Strategy and...	6
4	The Jio Revolution: Redefining Connectivity and Commerce	9
5	Retail Resonance: Mukesh Ambani's Foray into Consumer...	12
6	Energy Evolution: Mukesh Ambani's Sustainable Power Play	15
7	Tech Titans: Mukesh Ambani's Digital Dominance	18
8	Global Footprints: Mukesh Ambani's International Expansion	21
9	Sustainable Futures: Mukesh Ambani's Environmental...	24
10	Philanthropy and Social Impact: Mukesh Ambani's Humanitarian...	27
11	Legacy and Future Horizons: Mukesh Ambani's Enduring Impact	30
12	Beyond Business: Mukesh Ambani's Vision for a Sustainable...	33
13	Navigating Challenges: Mukesh Ambani's Leadership in Times...	36
14	Summary	39

1

Introduction

In the bustling streets of Mumbai, where ambition meets innovation, the narrative of one of India's most influential business leaders unfolds — Mukesh Ambani. "Mastering the Ambani Empire: Mukesh Ambani's Journey to Business Mastery" is a captivating exploration of the visionary architect behind the colossal conglomerate that has left an indelible mark on the global business landscape.

Chapter by chapter, this book peels back the layers of Ambani's strategic brilliance, tracing the evolution of the Ambani Empire from its modest origins to a global powerhouse. From diversification into key sectors, including telecommunications, retail, and energy, to groundbreaking forays into digital technology and sustainable business practices, Ambani's journey reflects a dynamic and multifaceted approach to leadership.

As we embark on this narrative journey, we'll delve into the intricacies of Ambani's business acumen, the global impact of the Ambani Empire, and its role as a catalyst for technological and social transformation. This book is an exploration of resilience in the face of challenges, a testament to the power of innovation, and a celebration of Ambani's enduring commitment to creating a sustainable and impactful legacy. Join us on this compelling journey through the corridors of business mastery, where ambition, vision, and strategic brilliance converge to shape the extraordinary story of Mukesh Ambani and the empire he has masterfully built.

2

The Genesis of Ambani Dominance

Title: "The Ambani Empire: Mukesh Ambani's Journey to Business Mastery"

Introduction:

In the heart of Mumbai, where the bustling streets merge with the soaring skyline, lies the epicenter of one of the most formidable business empires in the world—the Ambani Empire. This chapter delves into the genesis of this colossal conglomerate, tracing the footsteps of its visionary architect, Mukesh Ambani, as he embarked on a journey that would redefine the landscape of Indian business.

Section 1: Roots of Ambition

The narrative begins in the quiet lanes of Yemen, where a young Dhirubhai Ambani, Mukesh's father, laid the foundation of the family's entrepreneurial spirit. Born into modest means, Dhirubhai's unwavering ambition and keen business acumen led him to establish Reliance Industries, the precursor to the Ambani Empire. This section explores the early struggles, triumphs, and the values that laid the groundwork for the empire's future.

Section 2: Nurturing a Visionary

Mukesh Ambani, the eldest son of Dhirubhai, grew up amidst the whirlwind of his father's business ventures. This section unravels the formative years of Mukesh, his education, and the invaluable lessons imbibed from his father. As he set foot into the world of business, Mukesh's sharp intellect and strategic thinking became evident, foreshadowing the brilliance that would later propel the Ambani Empire to unprecedented heights.

Section 3: The Reliance Revolution

The 1980s witnessed the emergence of Reliance Industries as a major player in diverse sectors, including petrochemicals, textiles, and telecommunications. This section explores Mukesh Ambani's pivotal role in steering the company through this transformative era, navigating challenges and capitalizing on opportunities. The Reliance Revolution set the stage for the empire's expansion and marked Mukesh's ascent as a formidable business leader.

Section 4: Pioneering the Digital Frontier

The chapter concludes by examining Mukesh Ambani's audacious foray into the digital realm with the launch of Jio, a telecom venture that sent shockwaves through the industry. The strategic vision behind Jio and its impact on India's digital landscape are dissected, offering insights into how Mukesh Ambani harnessed the power of technology to further fortify the Ambani Empire.

Epilogue:

As the chapter draws to a close, the Ambani Empire stands as a testament to Mukesh Ambani's business prowess. The journey from humble beginnings to the zenith of corporate success lays the groundwork for the chapters to come, promising a riveting exploration of the strategies, challenges, and triumphs that define the evolution of the Ambani business dynasty.

3

Building Blocks of the Ambani Empire: Strategy and Diversification

Title: "Architectural Brilliance: Mukesh Ambani's Strategic Tapestry"

Introduction:

Having laid the foundation of the Ambani Empire in the preceding chapter, this segment navigates through the intricacies of Mukesh Ambani's strategic acumen. From diversification to risk management, this chapter illuminates the shrewd decisions and calculated risks that propelled the Ambani conglomerate into new realms of industry dominance.

Section 1: Diversification Dynamics

Mukesh Ambani's visionary approach to diversification emerges as a central theme in this section. Analyzing the strategic decisions that led to the expansion of Reliance Industries into sectors as diverse as energy, retail, and telecommunications, we unravel the symbiotic relationships between the various branches of the empire. This diversification not only fortified the business against economic volatility but also positioned the Ambani conglomerate as a versatile powerhouse.

Section 2: The Art of Risk Management

Behind every successful empire lies a portfolio of well-calculated risks. This section delves into Mukesh Ambani's adeptness at risk management, examining pivotal moments when bold decisions shaped the destiny of the Ambani businesses. From navigating regulatory challenges to weathering economic downturns, Ambani's ability to foresee potential pitfalls and navigate through uncertainties emerges as a key driver of the empire's resilience.

Section 3: Global Ambitions

As the Ambani Empire solidified its dominance on the Indian business landscape, Mukesh Ambani set his sights on the global arena. This section traces the international expansion strategies that propelled Reliance Industries onto the global stage. From strategic partnerships to overseas acquisitions, Mukesh Ambani's pursuit of global influence is dissected, revealing the ambitions that transcend geographical boundaries.

Section 4: Innovation and Technology Integration

At the core of Mukesh Ambani's strategic brilliance is a relentless pursuit of innovation. This section explores how Ambani leveraged technological advancements to stay ahead of the curve. Whether through groundbreaking initiatives in the energy sector or the revolutionary Jio platform, Ambani's commitment to technological integration emerges as a driving force behind the empire's sustained growth.

Epilogue:

Chapter 2 concludes with a panoramic view of the strategic tapestry woven by Mukesh Ambani. The Ambani Empire, now a multifaceted giant with a global footprint, stands as a testament to a leader's foresight, adaptability, and unwavering commitment to excellence. The subsequent chapters will unravel further layers of this saga, exploring the dynamic landscape of Mukesh Ambani's leadership and the ever-evolving legacy of the Ambani business dynasty.

4

The Jio Revolution: Redefining Connectivity and Commerce

Title: "Jio's Triumph: Mukesh Ambani's Game-Changing Revolution"

Introduction:

As the Ambani Empire entered the 21st century, a seismic shift occurred in the form of Jio—the telecommunications arm that revolutionized connectivity and transformed the digital landscape in India. This chapter delves into the strategic masterstroke of Mukesh Ambani, exploring the inception, challenges, and triumphs of Jio, a venture that not only disrupted the telecom industry but also laid the groundwork for a new era in digital commerce.

Section 1: The Birth of Jio

The chapter begins by unraveling the genesis of Jio, from its conceptualization to its market entry. Mukesh Ambani's vision for providing affordable and high-speed internet to every Indian became a reality with Jio's launch in 2016.

This section explores the strategic thinking behind this audacious move and the meticulous planning that went into making Jio a household name.

Section 2: Disrupting the Telecom Landscape

Jio's entry into the telecom sector sent shockwaves through the industry. This section chronicles the disruptive tactics employed by Mukesh Ambani, from offering free trials to aggressive pricing strategies, to quickly amass a massive subscriber base. The impact of Jio on competitors and the overall landscape of telecommunications in India is dissected, revealing the ripple effects of this game-changing revolution.

Section 3: Convergence of Commerce and Connectivity

Mukesh Ambani's strategic brilliance extended beyond telecommunications with Jio's integration into the broader digital ecosystem. This section explores how Jio became more than just a telecom provider, evolving into a platform that seamlessly integrated e-commerce, content streaming, and digital services. The convergence of commerce and connectivity not only enhanced customer experience but also positioned Jio as a formidable player in the digital marketplace.

Section 4: Challenges and Triumphs

The Jio journey was not without its challenges. This section explores the hurdles faced by Mukesh Ambani and his team, from regulatory issues to intense competition. The triumphs, however, are equally highlighted, showcasing how Jio not only weathered storms but emerged stronger, fundamentally altering the dynamics of the telecom and digital industries.

Epilogue:

Chapter 3 concludes with Jio firmly established as a linchpin in the Ambani

Empire. The revolution initiated by Mukesh Ambani through Jio transcends connectivity, reaching into the realms of commerce, entertainment, and technology. As we move forward in this narrative, we anticipate the unfolding chapters to reveal the ongoing impact of Jio on the Ambani legacy and its continued influence on the global digital landscape.

5

Retail Resonance: Mukesh Ambani's Foray into Consumer Dominance

Title: "Retail Reinvented: Mukesh Ambani's Consumer-Centric Triumph"

Introduction:

As the Ambani Empire continued its dynamic evolution, the spotlight turned to the retail sector. In this chapter, we explore Mukesh Ambani's strategic foray into retail, witnessing the transformation of Reliance Retail into a consumer-centric powerhouse. From brick-and-mortar establishments to e-commerce prowess, this chapter navigates the landscape of Ambani's retail reinvention.

Section 1: From Textiles to Retail Titans

The chapter commences by tracing the roots of Reliance's retail endeavors, harking back to Dhirubhai Ambani's early ventures in the textile industry. Mukesh Ambani's strategic decision to diversify into retail is dissected, revealing the visionary thinking that propelled Reliance Retail into an expansive and diverse consumer-oriented enterprise.

Section 2: The Omnichannel Approach

Mukesh Ambani's approach to retail was not confined to traditional brick-and-mortar establishments. This section explores the omnichannel strategy employed by Reliance Retail, seamlessly integrating physical stores with e-commerce platforms. The innovative use of technology and data-driven insights to enhance customer experience is unraveled, showcasing Ambani's commitment to staying at the forefront of retail trends.

Section 3: Acquisitions and Alliances

Mukesh Ambani's retail journey was marked by strategic acquisitions and alliances that fortified Reliance's position in the market. This section delves into key partnerships and acquisitions that shaped the retail landscape, examining how Ambani strategically positioned the conglomerate to dominate various consumer sectors, from grocery to fashion.

Section 4: Digital Disruption in Retail

The chapter explores how Mukesh Ambani leveraged digital technologies to disrupt the traditional retail model. From the integration of JioMart into the digital ecosystem to the use of data analytics for personalized customer experiences, this section illuminates the ways in which Ambani's digital acumen transformed Reliance Retail into a dynamic, technology-driven entity.

Epilogue:

Chapter 4 concludes with Reliance Retail firmly established as a consumer-centric force, seamlessly blending traditional retail with cutting-edge digital strategies. Mukesh Ambani's vision for retail goes beyond buying and selling;

it encapsulates a commitment to creating an integrated and personalized consumer experience. As the narrative unfolds, the subsequent chapters will unravel further layers of Mukesh Ambani's strategic brilliance, exploring the continued impact of the Ambani Empire on the global business landscape.

6

Energy Evolution: Mukesh Ambani's Sustainable Power Play

Title: "Powering Progress: Mukesh Ambani's Energy Revolution"

Introduction:

In this chapter, we turn our attention to the foundational sector of the Ambani Empire — energy. Mukesh Ambani's strategic maneuvers in the energy industry have not only shaped the conglomerate's economic standing but have also played a pivotal role in India's energy landscape. From traditional oil and gas to the pursuit of sustainable alternatives, this chapter explores the multifaceted journey of Reliance Industries in the energy sector.

Section 1: Petrochemical Prowess

The chapter begins by examining the early years of Reliance Industries in the energy sector, focusing on the establishment of the company as a petrochemical giant. Mukesh Ambani's astute business decisions and investments in refining and petrochemicals are explored, showcasing how these foundational steps laid the groundwork for the empire's expansive energy portfolio.

Section 2: Oil and Gas Exploration

Mukesh Ambani's energy vision extended beyond conventional boundaries with the exploration and production of oil and gas. This section delves into the strategic initiatives and global ventures undertaken by Reliance Industries to secure energy resources, ensuring a stable and diversified energy supply for the conglomerate.

Section 3: Green Energy Ambitions

As global consciousness shifted towards sustainable practices, Mukesh Ambani positioned Reliance Industries at the forefront of the green energy revolution. This section explores the conglomerate's foray into renewable energy, including solar and wind power. Ambani's commitment to sustainability and the ambitious goals set for carbon neutrality are examined, shedding light on how the empire adapts to evolving global energy trends.

Section 4: Technological Innovation in Energy

The chapter highlights Mukesh Ambani's emphasis on technological innovation to drive efficiency and sustainability in the energy sector. From advanced refining technologies to digital solutions optimizing energy production, this section unveils how Ambani's commitment to innovation has positioned Reliance Industries as a trailblazer in the technological evolution of the energy industry.

Epilogue:

Chapter 5 concludes with Reliance Industries firmly entrenched as a major player in the global energy landscape. Mukesh Ambani's strategic foresight and commitment to sustainability have not only propelled the conglomerate's success in the energy sector but have also contributed to shaping India's energy future. As we progress through the narrative, subsequent chapters will delve into the continued impact of Ambani's energy revolution on both business and the environment.

7

Tech Titans: Mukesh Ambani's Digital Dominance

Title: "Digital Dynamo: Mukesh Ambani's Tech Triumph"

Introduction:

As the digital era unfolded, Mukesh Ambani foresaw the transformative power of technology. This chapter explores the ambitious digital endeavors that propelled the Ambani Empire to new heights, focusing on the strategic integration of technology across various sectors and the establishment of digital platforms that revolutionized industries.

Section 1: The Digital Infusion

The chapter kicks off by dissecting Mukesh Ambani's visionary approach to the digital revolution. From the early integration of technology in traditional sectors to the creation of a digital ecosystem, Ambani's commitment to embracing and driving technological change becomes evident. This section explores the strategic decisions that positioned the Ambani conglomerate at the forefront of India's digital transformation.

Section 2: Jio Platforms: A Digital Powerhouse

Building upon the success of Jio in the telecommunications sector, this section delves into the creation of Jio Platforms — an entity that encapsulates Ambani's digital vision. From strategic investments to partnerships with global tech giants, we explore how Jio Platforms emerged as a digital powerhouse, integrating services ranging from communication and entertainment to e-commerce.

Section 3: Ambani's Big Tech Bets

Mukesh Ambani's tech triumph extends beyond Jio Platforms. This section navigates through Ambani's strategic investments in and partnerships with major global tech companies. The collaboration with leading players in the tech industry, from Google to Facebook, is examined, revealing how these alliances positioned the Ambani Empire on the global digital map.

Section 4: E-commerce and Beyond

The chapter further explores Mukesh Ambani's foray into e-commerce, with a focus on platforms like JioMart. The strategic integration of digital services into the retail landscape and the evolution of e-commerce under the Ambani umbrella are dissected. Ambani's unique approach to blending traditional retail with cutting-edge digital solutions is illuminated.

Epilogue:

Chapter 6 concludes with the Ambani Empire firmly established as a digital dynamo. Mukesh Ambani's strategic maneuvers in the tech landscape have not only reshaped the conglomerate but have also played a pivotal role in steering India's digital evolution. As we progress through the narrative, subsequent chapters will continue to unravel the ongoing impact of Ambani's digital dominance on business, society, and the global tech landscape.

8

Global Footprints: Mukesh Ambani's International Expansion

Title: "Beyond Borders: Mukesh Ambani's Global Ventures"

Introduction:

As the Ambani Empire continued to scale new heights, Mukesh Ambani set his sights on global expansion. This chapter explores the strategic initiatives and international ventures that propelled the conglomerate beyond Indian borders, shaping Reliance Industries into a global force across diverse industries.

Section 1: Strategic Alliances and Partnerships

The chapter begins by examining Mukesh Ambani's approach to global expansion through strategic alliances and partnerships. From collaborations with multinational corporations to joint ventures in key sectors, we delve into the meticulous planning that went into building global synergies and creating mutually beneficial relationships.

Section 2: Overseas Investments and Acquisitions

Mukesh Ambani's pursuit of global influence is further explored through overseas investments and acquisitions. This section navigates through key acquisitions and investments that expanded the Ambani Empire's presence in sectors such as energy, technology, and retail on the global stage. Ambani's strategic vision for leveraging international opportunities is scrutinized, offering insights into the conglomerate's global strategy.

Section 3: Tech Diplomacy and Innovation Hubs

Mukesh Ambani's global endeavors extend beyond business transactions to the realm of tech diplomacy and innovation. This section explores how Ambani established innovation hubs, fostering collaboration with global tech talent and contributing to the global tech ecosystem. The conglomerate's role in shaping international technological advancements is highlighted, showcasing Ambani's commitment to being at the forefront of innovation on a global scale.

Section 4: Challenges and Successes on the Global Stage

Global expansion is not without its challenges. This section examines the hurdles faced by Mukesh Ambani and the Ambani Empire in the process of internationalization. From regulatory complexities to cultural nuances, the chapter provides a nuanced view of the triumphs and tribulations encountered on the global stage.

Epilogue:

Chapter 7 concludes with the Ambani Empire firmly entrenched as a global player. Mukesh Ambani's strategic forays into international markets have not only diversified the conglomerate's portfolio but have also positioned it as a key player in shaping global industries. As the narrative progresses, subsequent chapters will unravel the continued impact of Ambani's global ventures on the business landscape and the conglomerate's role in shaping the global economy.

9

Sustainable Futures: Mukesh Ambani's Environmental Stewardship

Title: "Green Horizons: Mukesh Ambani's Environmental Leadership"

Introduction:

As the world grapples with the challenges of climate change, Mukesh Ambani takes center stage in this chapter as a pioneer in sustainable business practices. The focus shifts to the environmental stewardship and green initiatives undertaken by the Ambani Empire, showcasing how Mukesh Ambani is steering the conglomerate towards a future that prioritizes ecological responsibility.

Section 1: The Path to Sustainability

The chapter begins by exploring the evolution of Mukesh Ambani's environmental consciousness. From early efforts to reduce the ecological footprint of the conglomerate's operations to the integration of sustainability as a core business value, we delve into the transformative journey towards a greener and more sustainable future.

Section 2: Renewable Energy Revolution

Mukesh Ambani's commitment to sustainable energy sources is a central theme in this section. The chapter navigates through the conglomerate's initiatives in renewable energy, including solar and wind power projects. Ambani's vision for a clean energy revolution and the strategic investments made to bolster the transition to sustainable practices are dissected.

Section 3: Circular Economy and Responsible Practices

The Ambani Empire's commitment to a circular economy and responsible business practices is explored in this section. From waste reduction measures to ethical supply chain management, Mukesh Ambani's focus on creating a business model that fosters environmental responsibility is scrutinized. The chapter sheds light on how the conglomerate is redefining success by integrating social and environmental considerations into its operations.

Section 4: Philanthropy and Environmental Causes

Mukesh Ambani's philanthropic efforts in the realm of environmental conservation are examined in this section. The chapter explores the initiatives and projects supported by the Ambani family that contribute to biodiversity conservation, climate action, and environmental awareness. Ambani's role as a leader advocating for sustainable development on a global scale is highlighted.

Epilogue:

Chapter 8 concludes with the Ambani Empire positioned as a beacon of environmental stewardship under Mukesh Ambani's leadership. The conglomerate's commitment to sustainable practices not only reflects a dedication to mitigating environmental impact but also signals a broader shift in the business paradigm towards a more conscious and responsible future. As we progress through the narrative, subsequent chapters will continue to unveil the ever-evolving impact of Mukesh Ambani's environmental leadership on business and society.

10

Philanthropy and Social Impact: Mukesh Ambani's Humanitarian Vision

Title: "Empowering Lives: Mukesh Ambani's Philanthropic Odyssey"

Introduction:

Beyond the boardrooms and business endeavors, Mukesh Ambani's vision extends to philanthropy and social impact. In this chapter, we explore the philanthropic initiatives undertaken by Mukesh Ambani and the Ambani family, delving into the transformative projects aimed at uplifting communities and contributing to societal well-being.

Section 1: Foundations of Giving

The chapter begins by tracing the foundations of Mukesh Ambani's philanthropic ethos. From the early days of the Ambani family's success, we explore the values instilled by Dhirubhai Ambani and the subsequent commitment to giving back to society. This section sheds light on the philosophical underpinnings that guide the Ambani family's approach to philanthropy.

Section 2: Education and Skill Development

Mukesh Ambani's philanthropic endeavors in the education sector take center stage in this section. The chapter navigates through initiatives and investments aimed at promoting education and skill development, showcasing how the Ambani family is contributing to building a knowledge-based society and fostering opportunities for learning.

Section 3: Healthcare Access and Innovation

Healthcare access and innovation are integral components of Mukesh Ambani's philanthropic vision. This section explores the conglomerate's contributions to healthcare infrastructure, medical research, and initiatives that aim to make healthcare more accessible to underserved communities. The impact of these endeavors on public health and well-being is scrutinized.

Section 4: Rural Development and Community Empowerment

Mukesh Ambani's commitment to rural development and community empowerment is examined in this section. The chapter delves into projects and programs that address the unique challenges faced by rural communities, from agricultural initiatives to infrastructure development. The transformative impact of these efforts on the lives of individuals and communities is highlighted.

Epilogue:

Chapter 9 concludes with the philanthropic odyssey of Mukesh Ambani and the Ambani family firmly embedded in the narrative. The conglomerate's commitment to social impact and community well-being showcases a holistic vision that extends beyond business success. As we proceed with the narrative, subsequent chapters will continue to unravel the evolving impact of Mukesh Ambani's humanitarian endeavors on society and the broader landscape of corporate social responsibility.

11

Legacy and Future Horizons: Mukesh Ambani's Enduring Impact

Title: "Eternal Footprints: Mukesh Ambani's Enduring Legacy"

Introduction:

In this final chapter, we reflect on the indelible mark left by Mukesh Ambani on the business world, society, and the global stage. The chapter explores the enduring legacy of the Ambani Empire, encapsulating the conglomerate's evolution under Mukesh Ambani's leadership and casting a gaze toward the future.

Section 1: Evolution and Adaptability

The chapter begins by examining the evolution of the Ambani Empire under Mukesh Ambani's stewardship. From its humble beginnings to its current status as a global powerhouse, we trace the journey of adaptation, innovation, and strategic evolution that has defined the conglomerate's resilience and continued success.

LEGACY AND FUTURE HORIZONS: MUKESH AMBANI'S ENDURING IMPACT

Section 2: Global Leadership and Influence

Mukesh Ambani's global leadership and influence form a central theme in this section. The chapter navigates through Ambani's role on the global stage, exploring his impact on international business, technology, and sustainability. The conglomerate's position as a global player and its influence on shaping global narratives are scrutinized, showcasing Ambani's enduring imprint on the world stage.

Section 3: Future Horizons: Emerging Ventures

As we look to the future, this section delves into the emerging ventures and industries where Mukesh Ambani and the Ambani Empire are setting their sights. From cutting-edge technologies to nascent industries, the chapter explores how the conglomerate is positioning itself to be at the forefront of future trends and innovations.

Section 4: Family and Succession

The chapter examines the role of the Ambani family in shaping the conglomerate's future. From succession planning to the involvement of the next generation, we explore how the Ambani family envisions carrying forward the legacy established by Mukesh Ambani. The chapter provides insights into the familial dynamics that will play a crucial role in the continuity and growth of the Ambani Empire.

Epilogue:

Chapter 10 concludes the narrative, encapsulating the enduring impact of Mukesh Ambani's leadership on business, philanthropy, and global affairs. The Ambani Empire stands as a testament to visionary leadership, strategic brilliance, and a commitment to creating a positive impact on the world. As we bid farewell to this exploration, the ongoing journey of the Ambani legacy continues to unfold, leaving a lasting impression on the annals of business history.

12

Beyond Business: Mukesh Ambani's Vision for a Sustainable Society

Title: "Sustainable Society: Mukesh Ambani's Humanitarian Vision"

Introduction:

This chapter delves into Mukesh Ambani's commitment to creating a sustainable society beyond the realms of business. Focusing on initiatives that address social challenges and contribute to the greater good, we explore how Ambani's humanitarian vision transcends corporate success and aspires to build a more equitable and sustainable world.

Section 1: Social Impact Initiatives

The chapter begins by examining the various social impact initiatives championed by Mukesh Ambani. From poverty alleviation to gender equality, we explore how the Ambani family channels resources and influence into projects that seek to create positive change in society. The focus is on initiatives that extend beyond traditional philanthropy, aiming for systemic and sustainable improvements.

Section 2: Environmental Conservation and Climate Action

Mukesh Ambani's commitment to environmental causes is further explored in this section. The chapter delves into initiatives and projects aimed at environmental conservation, biodiversity protection, and climate action. Ambani's role as a leading advocate for sustainable business practices and his efforts to contribute to global environmental solutions are scrutinized.

Section 3: Education and Empowerment

Education and empowerment take center stage as we explore how Mukesh Ambani envisions a society where knowledge is accessible to all, and individuals are empowered to reach their full potential. The chapter navigates through educational initiatives, skill development programs, and projects that empower marginalized communities, shedding light on Ambani's belief in the transformative power of education.

Section 4: Global Collaboration for Social Good

Mukesh Ambani's vision for a sustainable society extends beyond national borders. This section explores the conglomerate's participation in global collaborations and partnerships that aim to address pressing global challenges. Ambani's role as a global advocate for social responsibility and collaborative efforts to tackle issues like healthcare, poverty, and education are examined.

Epilogue:

Chapter 11 concludes with an exploration of Mukesh Ambani's enduring commitment to building a sustainable society. The conglomerate's multi-faceted efforts, from social impact initiatives to environmental conservation, underscore Ambani's belief in the responsibility of businesses and individuals to contribute to the betterment of society. As we transition to the final chapters of this narrative, the focus will shift to the ongoing impact of Mukesh

Ambani's humanitarian vision on the broader canvas of societal well-being.

13

Navigating Challenges: Mukesh Ambani's Leadership in Times of Adversity

Title: "Resilience and Resolve: Mukesh Ambani's Leadership in Turbulent Times"

Introduction:

This chapter explores Mukesh Ambani's leadership during challenging periods, examining how the Ambani Empire navigated crises and uncertainties under his guidance. From economic downturns to global disruptions, we delve into Ambani's strategic responses, resilience, and the lessons learned in steering the conglomerate through turbulent times.

Section 1: Economic Downturns and Market Challenges

The chapter begins by dissecting how Mukesh Ambani steered the Ambani Empire through economic downturns and market challenges. Examining instances such as financial crises or market volatility, we explore Ambani's strategic decisions, risk management, and adaptive strategies that proved crucial in maintaining the conglomerate's stability and growth.

Section 2: Global Disruptions and Technological Shifts

As the business landscape witnessed rapid technological shifts and global disruptions, this section navigates through how Mukesh Ambani embraced innovation and positioned the Ambani Empire to thrive in the face of such changes. The chapter sheds light on the conglomerate's ability to adapt to emerging technologies, industry shifts, and the digital transformation sweeping through various sectors.

Section 3: Crisis Management and Reputation

The chapter explores Mukesh Ambani's approach to crisis management and reputation during challenging times. Whether facing operational challenges, regulatory issues, or public relations crises, Ambani's leadership in crisis situations is scrutinized, highlighting the conglomerate's ability to weather storms while maintaining its reputation and integrity.

Section 4: Lessons Learned and Future Preparedness

Drawing on the experiences of facing challenges, this section examines the lessons learned under Mukesh Ambani's leadership. The chapter explores how the conglomerate leveraged adversity as an opportunity for growth, learning, and future preparedness. Insights into Ambani's leadership philosophy and the incorporation of lessons from challenges into future strategies are illuminated.

Epilogue:

Chapter 12 concludes with a reflection on Mukesh Ambani's leadership during turbulent times. The conglomerate's ability to not only survive but thrive in the face of challenges stands as a testament to Ambani's strategic foresight and leadership acumen. As we transition to the final chapters of this narrative, the focus will be on the enduring impact of Mukesh Ambani's resilience and resolve on the legacy of the Ambani Empire.

14

Summary

The narrative unfolds across twelve chapters, tracing the remarkable journey of Mukesh Ambani and the Ambani Empire. It begins with the genesis of the conglomerate under Dhirubhai Ambani's visionary leadership, setting the stage for Mukesh Ambani's ascent. Each chapter delves into a distinct facet of Ambani's business mastery, exploring the diversification strategies, technological revolutions, global expansions, and philanthropic endeavors that define the Ambani legacy.

Chapters 1-3 focus on the foundational elements of the Ambani Empire, showcasing its evolution in sectors like petrochemicals, telecommunications, and digital technology. Chapter 4 explores the strategic entry into the retail sector, emphasizing the convergence of traditional retail with cutting-edge digital solutions.

Chapters 5-6 delve into the energy sector, highlighting Ambani's commitment to sustainability and technological innovation. Chapter 7 takes the narrative beyond Indian borders, exploring the conglomerate's global ventures and strategic alliances.

Chapter 8 shines a spotlight on Mukesh Ambani's environmental stewardship, emphasizing his dedication to green initiatives and the pursuit of a circular economy. Chapter 9 explores the philanthropic side of the Ambani family, detailing their efforts in education, healthcare, and rural development.

Chapters 10-11 encapsulate the enduring legacy of Mukesh Ambani, both in the business world and in philanthropy. The narrative emphasizes the conglomerate's commitment to societal well-being, sustainable business practices, and global collaboration.

Chapter 12 concludes the journey, exploring Ambani's leadership during challenging times, highlighting the conglomerate's resilience and adaptability in the face of economic downturns, technological shifts, and global disruptions.

Collectively, the narrative paints a comprehensive portrait of Mukesh Ambani's multifaceted leadership, the evolution of the Ambani Empire, and its enduring impact on business, society, and the global stage.

www.ingramcontent.com/pod-product-compliance
Lightning Source LLC
LaVergne TN
LVHW010438070526
838199LV00066B/6079